Why Children Need
BOUNDARIES

Why Children Need
BOUNDARIES

How Clear Rules and Healthy Habits will Help your Children Thrive

LOÏS EIJGENRAAM

Floris
Books

Translated by Barbara Mees

First published in Dutch as *Liefdevolle begrenzing*
by Uitgeverij Christofoor in 2017
First published in English by Floris Books in 2020
© 2017 Uitgeverij Christofoor, Zeist
English version © 2020 Floris Books

 Also available as an eBook

British Library CIP data available
ISBN 978-178250-636-2
Printed & bound by MBM Print SCS Ltd, Glasgow

 Floris Books supports sustainable forest management by
printing this book on materials made from wood that
comes from responsible sources and reclaimed material

CONTENTS

PART 1: CHILDREN AND BOUNDARIES

PART 2: BOUNDARIES AT EACH AGE AND STAGE

PART 3: HOW TO ESTABLISH LOVING BOUNDARIES

Part 1

CHILDREN AND BOUNDARIES

1. WHAT DO WE MEAN BY BOUNDARIES?

Boundaries play an important role in our lives, though we often think of them in negative terms. We think of them as inhibiting our freedom to act and so dream of throwing off their restraints. Particularly in the West, with its highly individualistic character, we are told to believe from a young age that there are no limits to what we can achieve, and in the era of globalisation we are encouraged to imagine a world without boundaries. But boundaries form part of healthy human development, especially in our early years. Besides marking out where we can and cannot go, they also establish what is appropriate behaviour and what is not. Boundaries contain us: they provide us with a sense of security and make us feel safe. This helps us to build confidence as we gradually get to know the world around us. Without them we would be overwhelmed. Boundaries also restrain us: through the rules imposed upon us by our parents and society, they tame and temper our more instinctual nature. This helps us to develop inner strength. Without them we would be at the mercy of the worst excesses of our character, lacking all self-control

9

and the ability to direct our own lives. Boundaries give us something to push against and just as often they push back. This is a healthy dynamic that makes us strong.

An awareness of boundaries and how to deal with them is therefore a vital part of our development. They help us become fully rounded human beings, teaching us how to interact with others and to adapt to society. The foundations for this are laid in childhood.

Children experience boundaries not only through the care of their parents and educators, but also by literally feeling their way around them: my bed extends here, my play-pen ends there, the garden, street, village or city, the world in which I live. These boundaries are also experienced through the rhythm of family life, for example getting up at a certain hour so that everyone is at school or work on time. Boundaries are also felt through the rhythm of the family's culture: annual celebrations and holidays. Being consistent when raising children, providing love, perseverance and predictability as the caregiver, allowing time for fun and play, as well as time to be bored, giving space for children to develop a personal taste in music and clothing: these are all ingredients that help children to build personal boundaries.

Boundaries today

In many countries around the world, people experience a great deal of freedom in their daily lives. We cross boundaries between nations daily and many people feel we are becoming global citizens. We can go on holiday three times a year. Our food comes from all over the world and every type of vegetable is available the whole year round. An abundance of information is at our fingertips courtesy of smartphones and the internet, and thanks to social media we have hundreds of 'friends' on Facebook and can 'talk' to twenty people at the same time on WhatsApp. Networking within and beyond our own personal circles is almost a prerequisite for operating in today's world. Infant mortality has fallen and advances in medical science mean we are living longer. Everything seems possible.

But whilst these innovations appear to solve certain problems, they also present us with other challenges. How long will the earth be able to sustain our way of living? Should my ten year old have a mobile phone and at what age should I allow them on Facebook? Nothing is straightforward. The certainties of just a few decades ago have vanished. Jobs are hard to find and long term, permanent employment can be even harder to come by. There is no longer any such thing as a job for life. And whilst we can apply for credit cards and take out loans to extend our finances when we struggle to make ends meet, this can all too easily lead us into debt from which it is difficult to escape.

All of these questions relate to boundaries, and today many people are searching for ways to create loving boundaries for their children that will help them thrive. We encounter this subject in the media and on the playground. In this book, we will look closely at how various types of boundary form the building blocks of healthy child development. Boundaries are not fixed but grow with the different developmental phases of the children entrusted to our care.

Ever-shifting boundaries

Many of the questions we face today concerning boundaries are quite new. It's easy to forget that until relatively recently, life was very different. Nowadays it is commonplace for women to pursue further education and a successful career outside of the home, and more men are choosing to stay at home to raise their children or play a larger role in home life in general. But if we look back fifty or sixty years we find the situation was very different. Fewer women attended university and in the workplace, opportunities for women were more restricted. They were expected to stay at home, tend to the house and look after the children. Husbands were the providers.

Looking back further to the nineteenth century, the Industrial Revolution brought about a radical transformation in the economic and social life of Europe. People began to migrate to the cities in larger numbers. Women, who up until then had taken care of the house and children and did what work was needed in their small communities, now for the first time went to work outside the home in factories. The first childcare facilities were established and, as a result, the first questions were asked about children's needs and rights.

Up until the Second World War, most children had a strict upbringing. Respect for authority was enshrined at the heart of the family and discipline was greatly valued. Children were expected to adapt to the rhythm and routine of the family: if they were hungry, they had to wait until it was time to eat, and crying was considered good for the lungs. In 1928, American psychologist John Watson wrote:

'There is a sensible way of treating children. Treat them as though they were young adults … Let your behaviour always be objective and kindly firm. Never hug and kiss them, never let them sit in your lap.'

After the Second World War, life for many people changed. The world had been shaken to its foundations, and many things that had been taken for granted before no longer offered security. Boundaries were broken and continued to be broken as countries rebuilt and a new world emerged from the ruins of the old one.

Then, in the 1950s, the ideas of the American paediatrician, Benjamin Spock, which he set out in his book *Baby and Childcare*, began to permeate society. In contrast to the rigid, authoritarian approach to raising children, Spock took a completely different view. He believed that all children had the best intentions at heart and that, whilst discipline was still important, parents should learn to trust their children. Spock's book had a place on thousands of bookshelves and was a great influence on the post-war generation.

Anti-authoritarian parenting flourished during the 1960s and 1970s. New research stated that children cried because they needed to be comforted and held in order to feel secure and protected. Parents were encouraged to let their children be free: if they were hungry, let them eat; if they were tired, let them sleep.

In 1989 the rights of children were defined by the United Nations and acknowledged by 196 countries. Among other things these state that, regardless of a child's background, race, colour or religion, they have a right to an education, privacy, an adequate standard of living, leisure, play and culture, and a right to have their views respected.

Over the past few centuries we have grown from people who lived in close communities with a group sense of awareness, into individuals with a very clearly defined sense of our personal self, our 'I'. We have become self-centred. Which raises the question: 'Is it possible to live as an autonomous individual within a community?' The tension at the heart of this question brings us back to boundaries and the role they play in our lives: both in terms of how clearly defined they are and how flexible they can be. The first allows us to enter confidently and respectfully into relationships with others, whilst the second allows those relationships to grow and develop without stifling individual freedom. Both are necessary for healthy human development.

2. SOME THEORY ON CHILD DEVELOPMENT

Rudolf Steiner, the Austrian philosopher and founder of the movement known as anthroposophy, from which Steiner-Waldorf education (among other initiatives) grew, provided a wealth of insight into human development that encompasses both the physical and spiritual aspects of our nature. Two aspects of Steiner's thinking are particularly relevant to the topic of boundaries and underpin a lot of the advice in this book: his descriptions of the 'fourfold human being' and the 'twelve senses'.

The fourfold human being

Steiner broke down the way we look at ourselves, describing people as consisting of four different levels of being: the physical body, the life body, the soul body and the 'I' or ego. Short explanations of these four bodies are given below.

Physical body
This is the body we are most familiar with, the one that can be seen and felt. It includes all the measurable physical reactions.

Life body
As its name suggests, the life body sustains all living processes within the physical body. It promotes growth, provides us with energy and helps us to heal and recover.

Soul body
This is the body of sensation that receives impressions from the world around us as well as from our own inner world: our thoughts, feelings and desires, both conscious and unconscious. All of these combine to form our behaviour.

The ego
This is our own unique individuality, identity, or personality – the spiritual core of our being that finds its expression over the course of our life.

The twelve senses

The development of a child, from birth through to their twenty-first year, is supported by a corresponding development of the senses. Anthroposophy recognises twelve senses in total and these allow us to examine the various stages of development in greater detail. They are divided into the bodily, feeling and cognitive senses.

The bodily senses
The bodily, or lower, senses consist of *touch, life, movement* and *balance*. These provide the soul with information about the body and pass information about the outside world inward. The *sense of touch* we know from the more standard

16

inventory of five senses. The *sense of life* deals with the functioning of the body. We notice this most acutely when something is out of order: when we are hungry or thirsty, or when some part of us is in pain. The *sense of movement* allows us to perceive our own movement, from raising our arms to blinking our eyes, and the *sense of balance* prevents us from falling over all the time. These bodily oriented senses form the foundation for sensorimotor development.

The feeling senses

The feeling, or middle, senses consist of *smell, taste, sight* and *warmth*. Through these senses, children not only learn to recognise their surroundings but also their perception of these surroundings.

The cognitive senses

The cognitive, or higher, senses are made up of *hearing, language, thought* and *ego*. These facilitate our spiritual qualities and allow us to be our unique selves.

The senses work closely together and are active throughout children's development and beyond. The four bodily senses form the basis of development for the feeling and cognitive senses, and play an important role in the early years of child development. Each stage of life works on forming and refining our senses. It is to these different stages that we now turn.

3. WHY DO CHILDREN NEED BOUNDARIES?

People say that love knows no boundaries.
But it is the boundaries that are the most interesting.

— Jean-Luc Godard

Building a safe inner space

All children are unique. With each stage of their development they awaken to a greater awareness of their own individuality, their own 'I'. This process takes place in two directions, an inner and an outer one. The inner direction deals with the child's emerging self-awareness, their experience of their inner world and their relationship to their own physical body. The outer direction deals with the child learning to adapt to the culture and society in which they live. As all parents know, this path is not a smooth one. With each new step the harmony that existed before is disturbed as a new balance is sought: the toddler becomes stubborn, the adolescent rebels. For this development to unfold in a healthy manner, it is important that the child feels safe and secure, both in themselves and in their relationships with their parents and educators. Establishing boundaries plays a vital part in achieving this.

During pregnancy and the first seven years of life, a child builds up the body in which they will spend their lives. The physical body is like a home for the child's 'I': it is made up of a foundation, walls, windows, doors and a roof. Every home is different, every child is different. Much like a house, our bodies are surrounded by a space in which we feel comfortable, like a garden. This usually measures about one arm's length around us and is experienced as our own personal space. Only people we trust and feel very comfortable with are allowed into this space, such as our partner, our relatives, or good friends.

This space is part of a child's inner world and is constructed by them with the help of loved ones. If a child is treated with love, respect, integrity and deference, they will begin to get a sense of this personal space which belongs entirely to them. This helps them to know their own boundaries, but also, as they get older, to know what the boundary of another person is, or what a socially acceptable distance is. A child will begin to have the experience: 'This is me and this is someone else' or 'This is mine and this is someone else's' or 'I can do this and someone else can do that'. Children need this inner space to stay in touch with how they're feeling and to reflect on their own experiences. It is also the space in which morals are developed in later childhood.

Building the foundations of morality

Children are not born with a moral compass. This is something they develop gradually over time by following the guidance of their carers. In his lecture series *The Spiritual Ground of Education*, Rudolf Steiner said, 'We do not endow children with moral impulses by giving them commands, saying that they must do this or that, or that such and such is good ... Children do not yet have the intellectual attitude of adults towards good and evil and the whole realm of morality, they must grow into it.'

Very young children do not learn by instruction but by imitation. In their early years, children are mimicking beings, imitating everything they see in their environment. If we want children to develop a healthy moral sense and a clear grasp of right and wrong, they need to see their parents and educators demonstrating such behaviour. We should not force moral judgements on children, but evoke in them a *feeling* for what is morally right and wrong, by encouraging what we consider to be good behaviour and discouraging more problematic behaviour. This feeling, if developed well, influences children's will impulses when they are older. In this way, Steiner says, 'we lay the foundation so that, when children awaken at puberty, they can form their own moral judgements by observing life.'

Developing social skills

As they grow, children encounter a variety of social situations. They must learn how to act appropriately within each one and understand what is expected of them according to the customs of their family, community and culture. The ability to do this is developed in the child's first seven years, during which time they imitate everything they see. Parents demonstrate to their children what is acceptable behaviour in any given situation and where the boundaries lie. This understanding allows children to handle social situations in a positive way and avoid negative consequences as much as possible.

Children also learn how to behave from feedback they receive. They experience, if unconsciously at first, that they receive praise and positive consequences from some behaviour, and stern words and negative consequences from other behaviour. Young children naturally want to please their parents, and positive consequences support inner growth and the development of self-confidence and individuality. However, this does not mean that children should only ever hear 'yes' and never be told 'no'. Children need to experience the boundary between what is considered to be acceptable behaviour and what is not; only then can parents help children to grow positively in a clearly defined, safe environment.

Children's ability to interact effectively with the world around them, and with themselves, grows through experience as they gradually develop an understanding of their environment and social relationships. What is considered socially acceptable behaviour becomes slowly ingrained in them and their responses to situations become automatic. This formation of social habits lays a solid foundation for their further development. They no longer have to feel wary of new or unpredictable environments because they know how to act in any given situation. They grow in self-confidence, and feel safe to lose themselves in play, for example.

Children who have been given few examples of how to behave in social situations do not feel as secure or confident. They have not learned how to deal with conflicts or how to reach agreement according to the norms and values of society. This can result in problematic behaviour, such as yelling and hitting.

Managing emotions

In order to learn how to act in social situations, children need a healthy self-image. This is achieved through knowing how to manage their feelings and emotions and learning to take pride in themselves.

Feelings and emotions can be seen as two different things. We can define feelings as sense impressions that arise usually through some form of external stimulus: for example, a sense of outrage at seeing litter being dropped in the street. Emotions arise internally, when our inner world is touched or affected in some way: for example, as a result of our hormones.

A good way to show children how to deal with their emotions is to consider how we as parents deal with our own emotions: what example are we setting? Are we quick-tempered or impatient? Do we jump the queue, interrupt conversations, or always want to win? Do we overindulge in chocolate, or shy away from facing the outside world? Everyone struggles to manage their emotions at times, but if we regularly react in a certain way, there's a good chance that our children will imitate our behaviour.

Fostering independence

Parents can foster their children's independence not only by focusing on what their children can do, but also by having a clear idea of what to expect from them at what age, and not asking too much. Parents can help themselves in this by trying to recall what was expected of them as children and what they were able to do at what age.

Clear boundaries are important in fostering independence. The more clearly parents can establish habits and rules, the more independent children will feel. This may sound contradictory at first; after all, how can laying down restrictions lead to greater freedom? But it is nevertheless true. The clearer the boundaries, the more children feel free to move around within them knowing they are safe and protected, which gives them strength.

Children gain in confidence through being able to do things for themselves, or when they receive just the right amount of assistance in something they cannot yet do entirely on their own. Babies who have learned to walk by themselves, experience: 'I can do this all on my own!' Children who are allowed to fall and stand up again on their own also learn: 'I can do this!' Children who fall and hurt their knees and then are comforted, experience: 'My parents helped me recover my balance, so I can accept my pain as well as the comfort I am given.'

Parents who develop warm, trusting relationships with

their children that allow them enough time and space to learn to do things for themselves, help to foster in them a healthy sense of independence.

Physical well-being

Physical well-being is all about how comfortable a child feels in their own body. Feeling comfortable in our own skin is a cornerstone on which to build self-confidence.

Physical ability plays some part in this. Children are rightly proud of themselves when they master a new skill: for example, learning to jump rope or ride a bike. If children are given the space and freedom appropriate to their age to move around, they develop a healthy feeling for what they can and cannot do with their body.

However, physical well-being encompasses not just physical ability but also learning to care for the body and keep it healthy. In this regard, it is essential that children learn to sense the condition of their body: for example, to ask for a drink if they feel thirsty. When secondary school children go to the supermarket during lunch break, they should know how to make sensible decisions when choosing what to buy. Buying sweets once is fine, but if they regularly take a sandwich to school only to throw it away to buy crisps and sweets later on their physical well-being will suffer.

Ensuring children are physically active, instead of spending all of their free time in front of a computer screen or television, is vital to physical well-being, as well as helping children to recognise when their body wants to be active and when it needs to rest and restore itself.

The more parents care for their own physical well-being, the better example they set for their children; and the better parents feel in themselves, the easier it becomes to make appropriate parenting decisions and spend quality time with our children. Good nutrition and regular exercise, sufficient sleep, an enjoyable social life, a little 'me time', and a healthy rhythm between rest and activity are all important for our physical well-being.

Material possessions

Educating children about material possessions is about teaching them the value of things – How much is enough? – and about 'mine and thine'.

How much is enough?
At some point, all parents are faced with the question: 'When is enough, enough?' How many toys should a child have? How many outfits? Which fads do we follow? The abundance of choice today and the challenges it poses to creating healthy boundaries for our children is discussed regularly throughout this book. It is a complicated subject, and there isn't a 'right' answer. Every parent must evaluate these matters as they arise and decide for themselves. No matter how many times they come up, the answers to these questions invariably lie in connecting with our own self-awareness – How much do we value material things? How grateful are we for what we have? – and drawing on our own inner strength. The more clearly we can identify our feelings on these matters, the better we

can demonstrate them to our children through our actions and behaviour.

Mine and thine

Children become attached to the things that surround them. They slowly develop a feeling for what is theirs and what is someone else's. This is my bear, my toy, my father, my mother. They are not yours! Children need these concepts to be able to understand and act appropriately in social situations.

This development starts with being overly protective and overly attached to belongings (and thus allows for a certain amount of egocentricity), and then progresses to the point where the child learns to share and even give away temporarily. Those of us who go through a healthy material development can still become attached to material things, but we can also see how the significance we invest them with is relative, transitory. The saying 'There are no pockets in a shroud' means there are no pockets to put our possessions so we can take them with us after death!

Part 2

BOUNDARIES AT EACH AGE AND STAGE

4. 0–7 YEAR OLDS

Supporting sensory development

During this early stage of life, children's bodily senses develop, which lay the physical foundations for all inner and outer experiences.

Through the *sense of touch*, children experience the boundaries of their bodies: I am here, the world begins there. They begin to experience objects, such as toys or the side of the crib, as being separate from themselves. From this, children gradually establish their own inner world and learn to differentiate between 'me and someone else', an important step in becoming an independent human being and developing a strong sense of self. Our skin is the organ that lets us experience the sense of touch.

Through the *sense of life* children experience how their body is doing: whether they are hungry, thirsty or tired. It allows children to recognise whether they feel at ease in themselves and with others, whether they are 'comfortable in their own skin', in harmony with themselves and the world. Paying close attention to children's signals from birth, and learning how to respond appropriately, helps them develop a strong sense of life. Children who receive this attentive care know that they can trust themselves and their environment.

The task of parents and caregivers is to care for all children's bodily functions so that they can sustain independently working organs each with their own purpose. This is achieved by, among other things, supporting the development of the senses.

The *sense of movement* develops primarily between the first and third year. During this phase children are busy learning to sit, crawl, walk and climb. Through falling and learning to get back up again children develop resilience. Through a healthy dose of frustration they develop will-power and perseverance, as shown when children learn to walk or in kindergarten when they learn to tie their shoelaces. If we look at learning to walk, every child does this in a unique way. If we leave children in a baby walker that keeps them upright, we deprive them of learning by trial and error, of achieving something all on their own. Learning to walk, ride a bike or tidy their rooms by themselves allow children to develop their will.

Parents offer a safe haven in which all of this can take place. The amount of space given depends on the age of the child, the parents' approach to parenting, and the circumstances in which the child is being raised. Over time children explore what is possible within the safe boundaries laid down by their parents; this safety net enables children to feel freer and more confident in discovering the world.

The sense of movement does not only relate to physical movement but also to a child's changing emotions and their capacity to be moved: a baby calms down when we sing, young children become restless when a storm is building, a story with lots of repetition gives toddlers and kindergartners exactly the predictability they need.

Just as children need to get a feel for their physical *sense of balance* when they are learning to walk or ride a bike, so too do they need to develop an emotional sense of balance in order to navigate the world around them. In this regard, as in so many others, all children are unique. Some cry more quickly than others, not because they are prone to overreact but because they are more sensitive: their inner equilibrium, or balance, is more easily thrown off. Some children never seem to get thrown off at all: they take everything in their stride. It's important to observe children closely and with love and empathy so we can establish rules and boundaries that support their own individual needs.

Developing social skills

During their early years, children experience a great deal of physical contact with others. They are continually being picked up and passed from pillar to post: from one relative to another, from one family friend to another. As children develop, they look for contact and start to communicate with those around them: a six-week-old baby consciously looks for contact with others through smiling. Older babies make sounds and react to sounds made around them. Toddlers make contact through imitation. If one of their parents sits on the sofa reading a newspaper, they will want to sit next to them and read together.

Kindergartners develop their social skills through imaginative play. Their play imitates what they have experienced 'in the real world'. Through play, they process what they do and do not like so that they can assimilate it:

for example, a visit to the doctor, or becoming angry at a doll or stuffed animal because their mother was angry with them the day before. During play, everything is possible because children know that it is make-believe.

Our habits around eating provide another way for children to develop social skills and adapt to the rhythms of the world around them. Babies learn that life has its rhythms: eating, drinking, playing, sleeping. Toddlers and kindergartners learn that we eat at certain times, and that eating is done together at the table and everyone helps in setting the mood.

Social skills allow children to make friends and maintain relationships. The following aspects all contribute to developing strong social skills.

Learning good manners

In a social context, contact with others is not a one-way street, there is communication back and forth, with each person ideally taking an interest in the other. This is known as *reciprocity*. Parents demonstrate this in the way they interact with others, thus showing their children important human values. And as we've already established, young children live and learn through imitation. Here are two examples:

EXAMPLE

After a day at work, one parent comes home; the other has been looking after the children all day. These parents have made it a habit to give their children a kiss when they get in, then the partner is greeted and they tell each other about their day while the children play together. Their parents set the example of asking each other questions and responding to each other. After that, there is time for the children to join in. The parents listen to the children tell them about their day and ask them questions that the children understand. This homecoming habit is a moment of peace with enough attention for everyone.

EXAMPLE

A different habit has evolved in another family. When the parents come home after their busy days at work, the children are first greeted extensively. They are the centre of attention. The same is true during dinner. Some of the children demand attention and interrupt when the parents try to talk to each other: 'Daddy, Daddy, I have to tell you something.' Not until the children are in bed do the parents have time for each other.

After a while, this ritual becomes draining and tension increases: the couple have become parents and educators exclusively and are no longer partners. The parents decide to try and break this habit, which is not easy but after a few weeks they feel that there is more space within the family. The children still receive plenty of attention but they have also learned to wait their turn. Both parents acknowledge that they had forgotten that they have various roles: that of partner, lover, parent and educator, and that all these roles need care. They both acknowledge that caring for their children has become more manageable. Now the house is filled with a different atmosphere of peace and genuine attention for all.

Parents who maintain and care for these different roles do so by laying down clear guidelines for their children. This then enables them to keep their relationship healthy and helps the children to develop their social skills through learning good manners.

Developing consideration for others

Learning to have consideration for others is dependent on being able to make inner space for another person. A three-year-old child is egocentric: they experience a world in which they are the centre. Not until children are three-and-a-half to four years of age can they start to play together and develop consideration for others.

When children are around three years old, they discover that they are unique individuals: they are an 'I'. This is such a wonderful discovery that they treat it as an incredible treasure that must be protected. In time, they discover that this treasure is here to stay and will not disappear. Only then can they open up to others and welcome them into their space.

The experiences children have with others help develop their confidence and their social skills. This includes disappointments. Social collisions with peers during play also teach them to put their thoughts into words, and to learn how to ask if they can join a game or play with a special toy. The more parents show their children to accept and learn from less positive experiences as well as good ones, the more resilient they will become, and the more they will learn to take others into consideration.

'Children encounter the world through the eyes of their educators,' Rudolf Steiner said. Parents who look at the world with deference, respect and love, and who approach their fellow human beings with these three values in mind, will show their children how to develop consideration for others.

The importance of free play

Play is something innate which children must do. A young toddler plays alone. At this age, children have so much to discover about themselves and the world around them that they do not have the energy or capability to also play with someone else. Older toddlers start playing next to their peers, and sometimes run into each other while playing. Soon they will take the first steps towards playing together: one child is the 'parent', the other is the 'child'.

Older kindergartners, five to six years of age, develop a more advanced form of playing together, which can be called imaginative or cooperative play. They plan together, collect everything they need and, while playing, the game develops. Not until later in their development will one child be in charge of the game and the other children agree to have one child in charge. These various types of play help build children's social skills. The only prerequisite is that children are given sufficient time and space for their play. Children whose schedules are filled with sports, music, ballet, play-dates and babysitters have too little time to play on their own. Valuing free play also means letting go, leaving children alone and not asking unnecessary questions such as: 'What are you doing? Are you having fun?' Children need the freedom to play independently without being disturbed.

One of the purposes of play is to process experiences.

During play, children can become someone else and this can help them regain their balance. For example, a kindergartner went to the doctor with an earache. The doctor examined the girl's ear with a lamp and then put drops in her ear. All this made a great impression on the child. Once home, the child's dolls and stuffed animals all had their ears checked. The child pretended to be the doctor and processed the experience through play. In another situation, she will be able to revert back to this moment. The more experiences are lived through and processed in play, the more children can learn from them. Positive memories help to create a sense of trust in the world. When trust in the world grows, self-confidence also grows and this provides a solid foundation for the development of good social skills.

Managing emotions

For children, discovering emotions is like discovering and exploring a whole world unto itself. They first experience the emotions of their parents and caregivers. From birth to around three years of age, these impressions enter children unfiltered: they have not yet marked out the boundary of their inner world and they soak them up like a sponge. As time passes, children experience more and more emotions themselves.

For the development of a healthy inner life, it is important that children learn to express their emotions clearly. Someone may say, 'I don't like what you just said to me,' but this does not describe exactly what they feel or mean. Parents who are aware of how they really feel will be able to teach this to their children. It is also important that children learn the emotional impact that words can have and not be careless with them. Children learn how to put feelings into words from age seven onwards. Until then, parents should do their best to sense the emotions of their child.

EXAMPLE

It is 5.00 pm. A five-year-old kindergartner has been at school and had a friend over in the afternoon. It's almost time for the friend to be collected and the parent lets the children know that they should start tidying up. The children look very busy, but they don't seem to tidy up. When the parent insists that they get going, the kindergartner says, 'I don't feel very well. I'm really tired.' The child is allowed to lie down on the sofa. Later in the evening, when the child is in bed, the parent tidies up. When reflecting on the situation, it occurs to the parent that the child said that he was tired regularly. It soon becomes evident to them that the child has confused the words 'I don't feel so well, I'm tired' with 'I really don't feel like tidying up'. This is not intentional, but is part of the child's exploration of the world of emotions.

Parents who tell their children that tidying up isn't always fun but is part of play, and who praise them when everything is neatly put away, help their children.

Children who do not want to tidy up but do so anyway, are assisted in the development of their will. Parents can help them through clear, constructive communication and not through communication that confuses them. This does not apply to very young children who at first can only imitate their parents' actions and habits.

Fostering independence

Knowing what children can do

Parents should not overestimate what their children can do, but neither should they underestimate what they can do. It is good to know what to expect of children and at what age. For example, healthy toddlers like and learn by repetition. This means that whilst sitting in a high chair, they will throw a playing block on the floor again and again. They do not do this to irritate their parents or to keep them busy! But because toddlers learn through repetition; they will repeat this game until they are sure that the block will always come back. They are developing trust. An older toddler can be expected to eat with a spoon without spilling their food. A six-year-old kindergartner can be expected to finish a task, such as setting the table.

Focusing on what children can do

The Hungarian paediatrician, Emmi Pikler (1902–1984), taught that even babies want to do things on their own. The closer the interaction between parent and child, the freer the child will be in their movements. We see this when dressing a baby. A parent who takes the time to tell the baby that they are going to be dressed in clean clothes, that this arm is going through this sleeve and that arm through that one, will notice that the child moves with them. When the baby is fed, they reach for the spoon as if saying: 'Help me to do this myself.' The 'terrible two's' is a phase in which two-year-olds want to do everything themselves: getting dressed, eating, climbing the stairs. Children at this age are proud and stubborn: they want to grow up but don't yet have the ability to know what they can do on their own and when they need a helping hand. It is important to handle these situations sensitively, so that children receive the required support without damaging their fledgling independence.

Material possessions

It's healthy for young children to have a phase in which they want to keep everything for themselves. They will not be able to let material things go until they understand them. It is essential for the healthy development of their understanding that children of around three-and-a-half years of age take care of material things. They must experience that 'this is mine and that is yours'. Taking care of their belongings is part of this learning process. Not having too many belongings is also important.

5. 7-14 YEAR OLDS

Supporting sensory development

In the early years of life children took possession of their bodies; now they are learning to feel at home in them, as their feeling senses develop. During this phase, children are mostly directed outward as their developing senses allow them to perceive the world around them. They learn how to act socially and deep friendships are formed. They discover their emotional life and begin to develop their own interests.

During this period, children continue to develop their *sense of smell* – they literally smell more. Around this time, children also start to develop their own moral sense. As strange as it may seem, these two things are closely connected: when something doesn't seem right to us, or is morally dubious, we say that it 'smells strange'. In the first phase of life children had no understanding of the concept of morality. Now, however, is the time to start cultivating a feeling for what is morally correct.

Between seven and fourteen years of age, children have developed their *sense of taste* so well that they can start enjoying their food. Their jaw has formed to the extent that they can chew well – the back molars have broken through and the rest of the teeth are changing. From six to seven years onwards, children start practising with making choices. Before now, asking toddlers or kindergartners what they wanted on their sandwich made little sense as they were not able to make such a choice. This is worth knowing if you want to avoid tantrums in the supermarket when you ask your toddler to choose between ten different desserts!

A figurative sense of taste also emerges during this period. For example, children develop a preference for sports, musical instruments, the authors of children's books, and other hobbies. They also develop a 'taste' for friends and form their own friendship groups. These groups influence the clothes they wear, what music they listen to, their social habits and so much more. The more parents have helped their children to develop their foundational, bodily senses during the first seven years, the better equipped children will be to continue prospering during this phase of life.

The *sense of sight* is about looking and observing. During this phase, children learn to observe more keenly. They see every detail and become more critical.

The *sense of warmth* allows human beings to feel the temperature around them as well as within them. Children need help until after adolescence in learning to assess their own sense of warmth and judging how many layers to wear. Too warm is rarely an issue in this phase, too cold often is. Setting loving boundaries also involves guiding children on the appropriate clothing to wear in various situations. For example, it's fine to wear a cropped t-shirt at home, on holiday or to a dance class, but that wouldn't be suitable clothing to wear to school. The clothes we choose to wear also allow us to express our unique personalities, and it can be difficult to balance allowing children sufficient space to do this with setting practical boundaries.

The sense of warmth is also about relationships. This is the phase during which children learn how deep friendships can be. They also learn how to maintain friendships and how important those relationships outside of the family are.

Developing social skills

During this period primary school children learn how to make and keep contact with others. They come to know what games other children like to play and learn to put themselves in someone else's shoes. These are all vital experiences that teach children what they can or cannot do and how to feel their way through situations. Around this time, they also start to discover their strengths, weaknesses and particular talents.

Children at this stage also become more aware that they are part of a larger whole. For example, there is food on the table every day thanks to many different people, but there are also many people in the world who do not have food on the table every day. This realisation and the example that parents set, help children develop greater social awareness.

Fostering independence

Whilst children may be eager to grow up, during the early part of this stage they still need a helping hand as they learn what they can and cannot do on their own. Nine-year-old children cannot be expected to remember to practise their instrument. Children at the end of primary school generally have the sensorimotor skills to mend a punctured bicycle tyre.

Material possessions

As mentioned in the previous chapter, children need to develop an understanding of mine and thine. These concepts relate not just to personal possessions, but also to social situations and the behaviour appropriate to them.

EXAMPLE

A couple enters a pizzeria together with their three sons aged between nine and fifteen. The restaurant is full and they have to wait for a table. Waiters hurry back and forth with plates piled high. The boys grab salt and pepper pots to use as guns as they play cops and robbers in the aisles between the tables. The parents don't react. They are both busy on their smartphones. One of the waiters asks the boys to make room for his colleagues. The father snaps at the boys that they should behave. The boys continue playing and nearly collide with one of the waiters. The chef asks them to stop. Again, the father tells them to behave without looking up from his phone.

I believe these children have not learned well enough, among other things, what *thine* is. A restaurant is a space that must be shared with others. It is not a playground and the aisles are not for playing tag in.

6. 14–21 YEAR OLDS

Supporting sensory development

From fourteen to twenty-one, young people really focus on developing their cognitive senses and shaping their own unique, free-thinking identities. Parents should try to model flexibility in thinking: how they arrive at thoughts, ideas and points of view, and how they amend these when necessary.

During this phase of life, adolescents further develop their *sense of hearing*. For this reason, choir is included in the secondary school curriculum of Waldorf schools. When put together, all the different voices create one sound, but this can only be achieved if everyone listens effectively to each other. Hearing and listening are not the same thing, however. Hearing is what our ears do and does not require a deep, inner connection: I can hear the kettle boiling in the kitchen. *Listening* is hearing with your heart, hearing with *attention*. It is about connecting yourself with the world.

For parents and educators who want to set loving boundaries, this sense is extremely important. Are we able to hear the question *behind* the question that our child asks us? And the same goes for our children, who, no matter what words we choose to say, can really *hear* what we think.

Their inner being *hears* our morality, not just our simple judgement of 'good' or 'bad', but also our sympathy for good and antipathy for bad.

The *sense of language* connects us with words. During the adolescent years, young adults develop the ability to express their inner world through words. Writing poetry or song lyrics or keeping a diary, anything that involves expression through language, is a great way to develop and share this personal discovery of language.

The sense of language allows the *sense of thought* to develop. This sense allows us to develop our own free thoughts and then express them in language. During this phase, we can start contemplating our own thought processes. Asking children to 'think about it' before the age of fourteen is setting them an impossible task.

The *sense of 'I'* crowns all the other senses. The sense of 'I' shows us what we are in essence. It is the captain of our ship of life and really knows what is best for us, especially in relation to our fellow human beings. Adolescents need to be given space and flexibility to develop their own sense of 'I' within safe and trusting spaces, which requires establishing appropriate loving boundaries that will vary for each individual. In order to judge what the right boundaries are, parents need to observe our children closely using all of our senses, which we can hone through self-awareness and self-education. Parents especially need a strong sense of 'I' – not an egocentric 'I', but a firm, confident 'I'.

Developing social skills

During adolescence, the development of social skills becomes most evident in the emergence of sexuality. Adolescents literally feel their way when getting to know themselves and each other! Independent social life increases. This is also the time when they learn to explore the world independently and gradually take charge of their own lives, free from their parents' control. Questions such as the following arise: How late can I stay out? How many times can I go out at the weekend? Can I drink alcohol? And at what age? Can I smoke? Can my girlfriend stay over? Adolescents need guidance and clear boundaries in order to stay healthy and safe, but establishing and negotiating them can be challenging.

Later on, adolescents start thinking about what they want to do with their lives: whether they want to study more, what career to choose. Their sense of self is growing and blossoming and they search for their place in the world.

Children who can make this journey towards independence gradually, in safety, and in harmony with their parents and peers, are likely to develop good social skills and a positive self-image.

Fostering independence

This whole phase of life focuses on gradually preparing adolescents to become independent, but they still need age-appropriate support. For example, a fourteen-year-old will probably need help to plan homework for the coming week, but may be able to cook for the family once a week. Everyone is different, and as adolescents grow into their own unique selves, the role parents have in supporting them relies more than ever on properly *hearing* them and engaging with them as individuals.

Part 3

HOW TO ESTABLISH LOVING BOUNDARIES

7. AN OVERVIEW OF PARENTING STYLES

Today, everyone's parenting style is different, but in order to gain insight into how we deal with boundaries we'll broadly divide the styles into four categories: free, strict, balanced and neglectful. It is unlikely that parents will identify with just one style.

Free parenting

Parents who follow this style cater to their child's every want. If the child doesn't want to do something, a discussion may follow about why not, what they want to do instead, and what the pros and cons of this decision are. The child is given a great deal of freedom in negotiating what they want, but it means that parents are often reacting to situations rather than taking the lead.

EXAMPLE

A little boy has just started school. On the second day, he is collected by his father. He doesn't want to leave and stays in the circle with his classmates. The father has already asked him a number of times to come, but he keeps saying 'no'. The father says, 'There are a couple of things we can do: we can go to the park and play on the swings, or we can go and get a nice piece of cake. What would you like to do?' The little boy doesn't want to do either of those things; he'd rather stay with his new friends. The father picks him up and the boy hits him in the face. The father reacts. 'I know you're upset and find it difficult to make a decision, but if you don't say what you want, I can't help you.' The boy starts screaming and they walk out of the classroom.

Parents who adhere to this style have very few rules or none at all, and almost everything is discussed with the child. The supposed advantage to this style of upbringing is that the opinions of parent and child are considered equal and there seem to be few conflicts because the child is allowed to do almost anything.

However, this style of raising children doesn't recognise the fact that young children don't yet have the faculties to make decisions. It therefore puts them in impossible situations to which they don't know how to respond, which can lead to conflict. Another disadvantage is that children do not learn the importance of boundaries. They experience little resistance or frustration, the two things that most help to develop a strong will. They do not learn to control their emotions or themselves, nor do they learn to take others into account: it's all about them. During adolescence, parents can lose what little influence they had on their children.

Strict parenting

In this style, parents are the boss. Rules are rigid and are not explained and children are expected to obey them or be punished physically or emotionally. The parents make almost all of the decisions for their children and there is no room for discussion or negotiation.

As a consequence, children develop neither the ability nor the confidence to explain, both to themselves and their parents, why they want something. They have difficulty making decisions for themselves and lack confidence, often becoming meek and anxious, as well as rebellious and aggressive as they try to free themselves from parental control. This style of upbringing results in many conflicts between parents and children. As adolescents, children may withdraw from their parents and start doing things secretly in order to break free from their strict rules. Parents have an enormous amount of power in this style of upbringing, which can easily be abused.

Balanced parenting

Parents who adopt this approach are sensitively attuned to their children's needs and interests. They can sense what and how their children are feeling, and they act accordingly. They establish clear boundaries and rules appropriate for their child's age and needs, but they also consider their children's wishes. Children are supported and stimulated, leadership is given and rules are explained. For example: 'It's cold outside, so we're going to put on your coat, hat and scarf.'

It is generally accepted that this style of upbringing gives children the healthiest environment, psychologically speaking, in which to grow up. They know what the rules are and what is expected of them. They understand what the consequences will be if they do not follow these rules – 'If you don't eat your dinner, you won't get dessert' – and therefore learn to be cooperative and develop good social skills. They are encouraged to do many tasks for themselves. This way they discover and realise their own competence and individuality, and develop self-confidence and independence. They are respected as unique people and their development is closely followed, with an openness between parents and children. Children tend to have fewer behavioural problems and are less susceptible to negative influence from their peers, both as children and as adults.

Disadvantages of this style are that children do not always obey, and discussing the 'how and why' of each situation and deciding how to respond can take a lot time. It's also hard to balance the parent/child roles. Children can become too assertive and continue to discuss and argue instead of accepting the boundaries laid down by the parent.

Another disadvantage is that parents can become so involved in their child's development that they start to micro-manage them. The well-being of their children becomes a project in which the children are enlisted in all kinds of clubs and activities that add to their rounded development and broaden their horizons. There's nothing wrong in this, as long as both parents and children still have enough time for themselves.

Neglectful parenting

Some children are neglected by their parents, to varying extents. There can be many reasons for this: parents might be overly busy, have addiction issues, or have experienced such neglectful upbringings themselves that they don't know how to raise children with love and care.

Parents who are overly busy

Parents are sometimes so busy with themselves, their career, or social commitments that they struggle to meet their children's needs. In many of these cases children are well cared for on a material level, but material objects are no substitute for a loving parental hug when attention and comfort are what's most needed. Parents miss out on asking their children how their day was and responding accordingly, and babysitters are not usually fully aware of children's needs. Later in life, when children look back on their childhood, they can feel as though they weren't important to their parents, they were always in second place.

Parents with addiction issues

When parents have addiction problems, which can manifest in the form of alcohol, drugs, gambling, sex or even gaming, all of their attention is focused on their addiction. Parents in these situations are often so emotionally damaged that they can no longer make room for their children or engage with their children's needs. Children of parents with addiction problems often have to cope with parents whose behaviour is unpredictable, and this causes them a great deal of anxiety.

Parents who had neglectful upbringings

Some parents are unable to care for children, often due to their own traumatic upbringing. They may neglect their children and give them little or no support. They may give very little guidance for their children to follow, set a poor example and be indifferent to the choices their children make. They may show no interest in them, be emotionally distant, and fail to provide a warm and comforting home for them. The children of these parents face loneliness and crave guidance and an example to follow. There is a good chance that the relationships they go on to make will be problematic.

EXAMPLE

A four-year-old boy is being registered at a primary school. Both parents and grandfather are present at the introductory meeting where it becomes clear that the grandfather raises the child. The parents live illegally with a friend in a one-room apartment. They are addicted to drugs and alcohol and the father is well-known to the police. As time passes, teachers at the child's school grow more worried. The school contacts the child-protection authorities, who have been looking for the boy for four years. He is not registered anywhere and has never been to a doctor or a dentist. Following this, the family moves to a different city without leaving a forwarding address. After a year, the family is located again and evidence of drug use is found in their apartment. The parents are placed under supervision and the boy is taken into care. The boy receives an extensive check-up that shows that his mental and emotional development have fallen behind that of his age group by two-and-a-half years. As far as the authorities know, this boy is the third generation to experience such neglect.

EXAMPLE

Two parents both have managerial jobs at a university hospital. They live in a big house in the middle of a forest about half an hour's drive from the nearest city, with a huge play room and a large garden with play equipment and even a swimming pool. They have two children, six and nine years of age. They have staff who take care of the house and an *au-pair* who looks after the children. She is the fourth *au-pair* in nine years. The family goes on holiday several times a year: skiing in Canada in the winter, safari in Africa in the summer, and a week on Bali during the spring holiday. The children are members of various sports clubs. They attend a school where parents are welcome at the many events and activities, such as plays and fairs, but the parents never show up, not even for parent-teacher consultations. The teachers are worried about the well-being of the children. One child has developed a nervous tic and is starting to fall behind in class. The overabundance of material things has not been able to make up for neglect on an emotional level.

Although these two examples may seem extreme, they both show types of neglect. Children who are raised in either of these ways do not experience the all-important care and boundaries needed for healthy development. They lack the positive role models of loving and attentive parents and they are denied constructive feedback on their own behaviour. They feel lonely and unloved. Children who have been neglected often struggle in social situations. They do not know how to be independent or how to build strong relationships and they frequently seek attention in the wrong way, in the wrong places and at the wrong times. They are unsure of themselves and suspicious of others, and as a result, they experience difficulty in finding their way in the world. Parents who are not capable of raising their children, for whatever reason, need professional support.

Multi-cultural parenting styles

It can be all too easy to judge parenting styles from cultures we are not familiar with, especially those that seem particularly authoritarian or permissive compared to our own. However, our society is becoming increasingly multi-cultural. If we want to live together in a fully functioning society, we have to learn to cross cultural boundaries. We have to ask ourselves who the person standing beside us is, and what habits and rituals are important to them and why. Only after understanding and celebrating these differences will we be able to break down the boundaries that have been raised between cultures through fear of the unfamiliar and the unknown.

Factors that influence parenting styles

It's not always easy to say which parenting style is most suitable because it depends on various elements, including:

Environment

Different standards prevailed in the Middle Ages. Likewise, times of crisis and scarcity call for a different approach to raising children than times of abundance. According to the 2018 annual report on global trends by the office of the UN High Commissioner for Refugees (UNHCR), there are nearly 71 million displaced people around the world. Among them are nearly 26 million refugees, over half of whom are under the age of eighteen. Many of their parents will have imagined a different environment for them than what refugee camps can offer, but they have no alternative.

Gender

Even though parents may not want to be influenced by gender stereotypes, many say that they treat their children differently because of their gender. For example, parents may not want their daughters going out on their own at night and insist that they come home with friends, whereas sons often have much greater freedom.

Socio-economic status

Children who grow up in lower socio-economic communities generally experience fewer opportunities than those from more affluent neighbourhoods.

However, some more affluent parents believe that their children's misfortunes can be solved with money, rather than educating them to take responsibility for their actions and teaching them how to deal with difficult situations.

Changing your parenting style

There is no such thing as the perfect parenting style. Many parents recognise themselves in the 'balanced' style. Often parents switch styles in temporary situations, such as a holiday, or during times of sickness or stress.

8. EVALUATING YOUR OWN BIOGRAPHY

This is the true joy in life, the being used for a purpose recognised by yourself as a mighty one; the being thoroughly worn out before you are thrown on the scrap heap; the being a force of Nature instead of a feverish selfish little clod of ailments and grievances complaining that the world will not devote itself to making you happy.

– George Bernard Shaw

The way we were raised serves as the basis for the rest of our lives, and influences the way we raise our own children. Perhaps we look back on our childhood with gratitude and joy. Perhaps we're not happy with the choices our parents made. The present parenting generation sometimes wants to do things completely differently from the previous generation: they make a conscious choice to change. However, engraved into our being are views, values, attitudes and assumptions and patterns of thought that we've learned from our parents, of which we may only be dimly aware. These determine how we will raise our children. To understand our partner, and therefore each other as parents, it's important to look back on how our childhoods have shaped our adult lives. Partners will always bring different parenting ideas and they should be embraced. However, if the differences are too great, they may cause a rift between parents causing the children to be faced with a conflict of loyalty. Keeping communication open and telling each other about past experiences is vital in creating a loving and supportive environment and helps both parents meet the challenges that lie ahead. Below is a list of questions that may help start a conversation about childhood.

(Grand)parents

✳ What do you know about your (grand)parents? How did they live? How were they raised? What standards and values did they have? What pearls of wisdom did they uphold whilst raising their children?

Childhood

✳ How do you look back on your childhood? What do you still consider to be valuable? What would you rather leave behind? What is characteristic about your family? What is a precious memory you have of your father and your mother?

✳ What style of parenting did your parents use? Was one parent more in charge than the other? What were your parents' views on punishment, rewarding, spoiling?

✳ Were you given room to discover and experiment? Were you allowed to be bored, angry, frustrated?

Were you allowed to cry? Did people shout at home? Did they swear?

* Did your family have rituals? If so, which rituals do you cherish and would you consider introducing them into your own family?

* What was your bedroom like? Did you share it with a sibling? Did you have a regular bedtime? Did one of your parents read you a bedtime story? Did they sing to you or pray with you? Did you feel safe in your bed?

* What toys did you play with? Where did you like to play most? Inside or outside? What did you play? Did you watch television? How often and for how long? Which programmes did you watch?

* Did you have friends? Did they come over? What did your parents think of your friends? Did you have arguments with your parents when you were an adolescent? What were they about?

* What do you know about your partner's childhood and upbringing? Are there similarities with your childhood? What are the differences? Do you have a similar cultural background?

* What aspects of your cultures do you want to pass on to your children? And which would you rather not give them?

Your child's grandparents

✳ What qualities do their grandparents have that complement your qualities as parents? Do the grandparents have to follow your style of parenting or can they deviate from this?

Your approach to parenting

✳ What is your view of the world and of humankind? What are your partner's views on the same? What parenting style most appeals to you? What are your views on boredom and indulgence, and the importance of frustration and developing resilience?

✳ What are your views on setting boundaries around the numbers of toys a child should have, the sorts of clothes they should wear and the type of food they should eat?

✳ How do you view your role as educator? How do you view your partner's role as educator? Does your child have more educators than just yourselves, for example leaders at day care, or teachers at school? What is their role?

The above list is by no means exhaustive. Add other questions you feel should be included and explore yours and your partner's backgrounds, where you both come from and where you are going together.

9. PARENTING BEHAVIOUR TO AVOID

Where you stumble, there lies your treasure.

– Joseph Campbell

Reconnecting with your child

At some point in their lives, all parents feel lost. They can't decide how to respond to their child and they may even feel that they've lost their close inner relationship with them. If this feels familiar to you, then maybe the list below can help you to re-establish that connection:

* Look back at pictures of your child and remember the times when you were deeply moved by how perfect they were; how pure, warm, endearing and completely dependent on you. What moved you then? What did you feel? How did you interact with your child?
* Pick up one of your child's favourite picture books and flick through it. This might bring you back in contact with the intimate bond you had.

✳ Sit on the edge of your child's bed and watch them while they sleep. Look closely. Try to see the innocent little child again instead of the 'impossible' one they have become.

✳ Write a letter to your child. You can choose to give them the letter – depending on your child's age and the contents – or you can choose to keep it or burn it. Writing can help put thoughts and feelings into perspective and may help you achieve new insights.

Raising children is a journey that you make together, a journey that lasts at least twenty-one years until the child, then an adult, takes up the reins of their own development.

Behaviour to avoid

When starting out on the long journey of raising your child, there are some traits and behaviours that, as parents, we should try to avoid. The ones we'll explore here are: the use of force, power struggles, being overprotective, controlling behaviour, punitive warnings, threats, yelling, reinforcing poor behaviour, overindulgence, asking 'why' questions, giving vague messages, and asking questions to which you already know the answer!

Force
Force can take the form of coercion, blackmail, physical violence or manipulation. Parents who exude authority and inspire trust don't have to force their children to do anything. Children may complain, but they accept the

daily routines and instructions as a matter of course. It's important that parents' authority should not waiver.

Power struggles

Power struggles seem to have one winner and one loser, but in the end both parties lose. A power struggle is kept alive by both the parents and children. Parents who have been pulled into a power struggle with their children should try to take charge again as soon as possible.

Being overprotective

Children need space to develop. They need space to fail, to experience disappointment, to feel grief, to waste time and so on; all of these are essential learning opportunities. Give your children the amount of space that feels right for their particular stage of development.

Control

Parents start controlling their children when there is a lack of trust and truthfulness, usually on both sides. Raising children is built on a relationship of trust, self-awareness and independence that grows and adjusts with each phase of development. Parents who feel they have to control their children should look more closely at these qualities in themselves and see where they need to work to improve them.

Punitive warnings

'Watch out! Be careful! I told you to be careful! Now it's too late!' Children who run around and discover the world will fall or bump their noses. They don't do this on purpose, or to hurt themselves, but usually because they are not yet aware of the consequences of their actions. Children feel hurt and confused if their actions result in unnecessary punitive warnings.

Threats

Threats and punitive warnings are connected. Threatening with punishment is a weakness that diminishes the parents' loving authority. Parents who threaten, raise children who will also threaten. For a child, making threats includes saying things like: 'I'm not going to do that! You can't make me!' or 'I'm going to live with Daddy if you are so mean.' Threatening creates a fraught and fractious environment.

Yelling

Yelling is not generally acceptable in our society – for example, it wouldn't be acceptable to yell at work – so we should not model this behaviour. Although sometimes it's hard for parents to control their temper, yelling does not work either in the relationship between parent and child, or between children themselves. It only leads to children being ostracised from their environment.

Reinforcing poor behaviour

Both positive and negative behaviour can be reinforced. Whilst it is good to reinforce positive behaviour, a child who is rewarded for negative behaviour will just as quickly repeat it. This is seen in supermarkets on a daily basis: a child takes things from the shelves and puts them in the trolley, even though they know this is against the rules. The parent admonishes them and they start yelling and screaming and throw themselves to the ground. Eventually, the parent gives in and lets the child have what they want. The child now knows that if they yell and scream they will get what they want. Success is guaranteed next time.

Overindulgence

Overindulgence ruins inner strength and burdens the rest of life's journey. See the following chapter where this topic is dealt with in more detail.

'Why' questions

'Why did you do that?', the mother growls to her five-year-old who has come home with a tear in their trousers. The child fell off the pavement. Why? The child has no idea. This question is laden with negativity: the child has to give a reason for something they don't have a reason for. Why? Because!

Parents could ask the same question in a different way: 'Do you know what happened to your trousers?' The child can then give a much better answer and the parent and child stay in loving contact.

Vague messages

One of the most difficult things about communication is saying what you want to say clearly. People often don't say what they really mean – if you listen carefully, you will hear many vague messages. This is not done deliberately: learning to actually say what we mean or feel or want is a life-long project.

Vague messages, like all those exasperating 'why' questions, are unhelpful when raising children. Comments such as 'be normal' or 'figure it out yourself' do not provide children with the clarity they need in order to understand what's expected of them. Parents who make clear how they feel and connect that with their child's poor behaviour, speak a language that their children can understand.

Asking questions to which you already know the answer!

Children need to learn how to communicate clearly so they can make themselves understood. Communicating with each other is a learning process and parents who practise this, who communicate clearly in order to create a connection, give their children a great gift. However, sometimes our messages have a double meaning, if they are suggestive or are questions to which we already know the answer. For example, a father and son are in a restaurant. The waiter comes and asks them what they would like to order. The father says, 'You don't want a milkshake, do you? You don't like milkshakes at all!' 'Yes, I do!' yells the boy. 'Don't yell!' the father yells back. He says to the waiter, 'He doesn't know what he wants. Come back in a few minutes.' This example illustrates asking a question to which you already know the answer and thus not taking your child seriously. The little boy didn't understand the father's joke at all.

10. AM I SPOILING MY CHILDREN?

Everyone has encountered a spoiled child at some point: one who is allowed everything, who whines and always get their way (picture Veruca Salt in *Charlie and the Chocolate Factory*). Of course, it's difficult to pinpoint what equates to 'spoiling' because a little indulgence here and there doesn't cause problems. However, when parents and carers are regularly too lenient it can have negative consequences for their children, resulting in issues such as:

* Children having an air of entitlement and unrealistically high expectations of how others should treat them.
* Having a low tolerance for discomfort, especially when caused by frustration, boredom, disappointment, delay, or when they do not get their way. This is often expressed through tantrums as well as verbal and physical violence.
* Finding it hard to develop strategies for coping with negative experiences.
* Being self-centred and believing that they're the centre of the world.
* Blaming others for their problems or expecting others to solve them.

✳ Not taking responsibility for the consequences of their actions or accepting the sometimes harmful effects they can have on others.

✳ Having no empathy.

✳ Finding it difficult to feel sorry for their behaviour.

✳ Demanding attention, not only from their parents, but from everyone around them. The more they receive, the more they demand.

✳ Struggling to socialise, especially at school, because they have not learned to deal with social structures or to accept authority, such as that of a teacher.

✳ Being chronically unhappy, angry, fearful or emotionally unstable; they often have low self-esteem.

Such children may seem to have a behavioural or emotional disorder, even though there is no measurable biological, genetic, physiological, developmental or other reason for their difficulties. When we delve further into this problem, we encounter three areas of indulgence: material, behavioural and emotional.

Material indulgence

When looking at material indulgence, the following questions arise: How many toys, how much pocket money, how many outfits or other material objects does a child actually need? How much time should lapse between wishing for something, such as a scooter, and actually getting it? How often does something need to be replaced, for example a mobile phone? Do we have to follow the latest trends? Should we reward our children with gifts? Whatever the parents decide, their decision often reflects their style of parenting and their world view. Children must learn to value and take care of their material possessions, for example, their toys. To do this, they must become attached to their toys and it is impossible for them to form this attachment (and thereby develop a sense of their value) if they have too many.

Behavioural indulgence

Parents who indulge their children in this way often do so out of a feeling of helplessness towards their children. They tend to act out of self-interest or laziness because they don't want to have to deal with another tantrum when their child does not get what they want. They are always able to justify their own or their children's behaviour, or their behaviour is played down and others are given the blame. They can be slow to act when action is needed, and often the way they do react to their children is arbitrary and impulsive, instead of being predictable and reassuring.

Part of establishing healthy, loving boundaries means looking critically at such indulgence. Healthy childhood development does not only mean 'not being ill'. It also means cultivating and strengthening children's will, developing their ability to solve problems and learning to accept things that are not as they might otherwise wish them to be. It is about teaching them to have consideration for others and how to be cooperative. These qualities are developed when the child is *not* spoiled.

Emotional indulgence

Parents who spoil their children emotionally give them too much positive attention at times when they should be more critical towards them; they display too much warmth. Positive warmth in a parent/child relationship has a down-to-earth coolness about it, whereas when a child is indulged this creates an oppressive warmth. By creating predictable habits within a family, by setting out clear boundaries for behaviour, the warmth and intensity of the child's wishes and desires are balanced by the parents' more predictable, measured coolness. This strengthens children's resilience and self-awareness.

As they develop the sense of balance, children quite literally lean on their parents. In an unhealthy parent/child relationship, the parent also leans on the child, meaning neither can develop themselves freely in the world.

Indulgence happens in all prosperous countries. For example, in China, where there was a one-child policy for some time, people speak of 'the little emperor syndrome' to describe only children who are worshipped by their parents and grandparents.

Willem de Jong (2013) came up with four questions that help us recognise indulgence:

※ Is the child hindered in learning tasks that fit their age and development?
※ Is a disproportionate amount of money, space, time, energy or attention given to one or more children in the family?
※ Do the parents benefit more from their actions than the child?
※ Is the child's behaviour damaging for others or society?

Children who, through parental indulgence, sidestep challenges in their development, will be confronted with these challenges sooner or later, only then they will be more difficult to deal with. When children are raised in a healthy way, habits are formed that are appropriate for their age and stage of development. Depriving children of this proper development through indulgence is investing in the short term and will lead to frustration for children later in life. Parents who spoil their children for their own benefit will eventually have to deal with the problems this causes. Children need parents who lead with a vision, instead of letting the wishes of the children lead the way. Children want a captain to guide their ship over the seas of life. Not until they are twenty-one can they take over the role of captain and call upon their own abilities as helmsmen.

Why do parents spoil their children?

When the first child is born, parents have high ideals about parenting and how to raise a child. As time goes by, they realise that these ideals must be adjusted. The phrase 'to raise' is a verb, it is an active process. During this process, parents realise that their role involves a lot more than they initially thought. They are parent, cook, protector, guide, fixer of things, peace-keeper, police officer, coach. Almost all parents want to give their children love, to protect them, care for their health and help them to be happy. But making children happy does not mean spoiling them; it requires a never-ending process of finding the right balance between the inner world, the outside world and the interaction between the two.

There are many reasons why parents spoil their children. A number of them are considered below.

Feelings of guilt

There are many parents who feel torn between the ideal image of the parent they wish to be and the reality of actually being a parent. Ideally, they want to be there for everyone and be good at everything, a Super Mum or Dad. In reality, this is impossible.

When they embark on raising a family, many parents don't realise how much time, effort and attention it will take up. Not only do they want to have the perfect family, but they also want to be a good partner, have a large group of friends, pursue their hobbies and spend time with their extended families. When it becomes clear that this isn't possible, many parents feel that they fall short and feel guilty.

These feelings of guilt can lead parents to spoil their children. Sometimes giving in to children seems to solve a problem. However, this is a short-term investment that only temporarily keeps the peace.

Separation and divorce

No one wishes for their relationship to break down and end, but it is an unavoidable fact of life for many families. Nevertheless, when relationships do end, either in separation or divorce, children often become spoiled. Parents feel guilty for the pain and grief they have caused their children and are more likely to indulge them as a result.

Competition is also a well-known phenomenon between divorced parents, with one parent allowing what the other will not. This is not in the best interests of the children. Even though parents divorce, they are still their children's primary educators; we can never become ex-parents or ex-educators. Children never become ex-children. Divorce hurts, but spoiling only adds to the pain.

Overly rewarding

Although every child is unique and brings something different to this earth, there seems to be a growing trend towards overly rewarding children, paying them compliments that are out of all proportion for the things they have done; putting children on a pedestal for being extra unique and extra special.

I once watched my children pass their swimming exams and was baffled by what I saw. When I was young, children went to the pool, swam, got their certificate, went to the locker room, got dressed and went home. No parents watched. It was nothing special. Today, the pool is decorated, there is music and every parent is ready to take pictures of their loved ones while they swim. The café prepares French fries and other yummy treats for the children, who receive gifts for having passed their exam. Is this healthy? Should we celebrate having learned to swim in this way? What kind of celebration will parents then have to prepare when their children pass their school exams and graduate from high school?

Becoming superstars

Every child has certain qualities, talents and skills. Every child can also be rude and behave inappropriately. Not every child can be the next Mozart, J.K. Rowling or Lionel Messi. Those on the podium need an audience to applaud them, and the vast majority of children will grow up to be part of that diverse, interesting audience. And yet it seems that in our times every child is encouraged to be a star. Children's uniqueness seems to have become a goal in itself for parents. Is this compensation for something that parents miss in themselves? Are we really concerned with the healthy development of our children, or are we asking too much of them?

11. FORMING POSITIVE HABITS

When bringing up children, parents are faced with a bewildering number of decisions, and there is almost always a moment, looking back, when it becomes clear that another better choice could have been made. It's very easy to establish habits and patterns of behaviour that are not conducive to healthy child development, but these can be broken if parents use their I-power, their own inner strength and self-confidence. Below, there are various possibilities to help change direction.

Let your child play

Free play, in which children engage in self-directed play without outside guidance, is a wonderful way to redirect indulgence by encouraging more independent activity. This play should take place without keeping track of time, without coaching from the parents, or without them playing referee.

Slowly build up the time your child plays on their own. If this is difficult for them, start with only five minutes. Tell them that they are going to play on their own now and that you are going to do something as well, for example, the laundry or some other household task. They may want to help you, depending on their age, and this is where you establish another healthy boundary: you say you will let them help you for a certain length of time and then they must go and do something for themselves. After this time of play and work, parent and child can spend time together, perhaps reading a book. As days pass, lengthen the time that the child plays alone.

It can take six weeks to break old habits (Schoorel, 2014). By gradually building up free-play time, children who are used to being entertained learn to create their own play. The parent has faith in the child and makes proper use of healthy, loving boundaries.

Have dinner together five times a week

Sitting at the table, enjoying a meal, talking through the events and experiences of the day all form the basis for good communication and a strong sense of 'togetherness'. Children may also experience that dinner is when their parents tell each other about their day. They learn that dinner time must be shared and that the conversation is not only about them.

Get rid of performance-driven pressure

We live in a time of performance-driven pressure, when even the smallest deviation from the perceived norm can cause parents to become anxious about the healthy development of their children. A perfectly contented eighteen-month-old child who does not yet walk suddenly becomes a child who has fallen behind in their development.

Children are adversely affected by performance-driven pressure. They can lose confidence in themselves when compared to others and feel that their individuality no longer counts. For example, one child does not understand arithmetic yet, but plays the violin beautifully. Another child is not good at language yet, but has a strong social awareness of everything that happens to other children in the class. Both children have valuable qualities that should be allowed to shine in the family, classroom or school.

We can take away this performance-driven pressure by carefully observing children. This enables parents and educators to see what is needed for each individual child so that they can help them on their path of development. Removing this pressure also means allowing children to be compared only with themselves and not with those around them.

Everything that is given attention will grow, this includes children when they receive positive attention.

Stop being overprotective

Being overprotective is gruelling and does not make parenting any more inspiring. Overprotectiveness creates people who have not had the chance to learn through trial and error. They have not had the chance to develop inner strength. Overprotectiveness can be stopped by observing closely if the child has a shortage of vitamins F and R.

Education must be unpleasant, confronting, it must interrupt, as I call it. Not to oppress or restrict children but to free them from their own desires and longings.

– Gert Biesta

Vitamin F and vitamin R

Vitamin F stands for 'frustration' and vitamin R stands for 'resilience'. Both can help prevent spoiling and over-protectiveness.

Children need a healthy dosage of frustration to build resilience, and resilience is required in order to persevere in the face of adversity, to be able to get up and try again. They develop resilience when they have to bike to school through the rain instead of being driven in the car, or when they have to save for something rather than just being given it. Children experience pride in themselves for carrying out what they have promised to do. It's also important that children experience failure and that they are honest with themselves and with others when they have not succeeded at something. This also strengthens the will in that it allows them to stay grounded and remain open to others, rather than trying to hide away in embarrassment or a misguided sense of shame at their failure.

Parents who attempt to keep frustrations away from their children are sometimes called 'helicopter parents'. This describes overprotective parents who take an excessively close interest in their children's experiences. They are referred to as helicopter parents because they are continually hovering around their children in an effort to oversee everything they do and help them avoid any problems. The psychologist

Dolf Kohnstamm recommends that overprotective parents practise 'loving negligence', that they allow children to be bored, giving them room to be naughty, and letting them get dirty, even bruised to some extent, in their encounters with the world. It means giving them room to solve problems.

Let children solve their own boredom

I experience boredom if a certain subject, person or situation does not interest me and I lose connection with them. This engenders a certain pain because I realise that I am not true to myself or the situation at that moment; I miss the feeling of connection between myself and the other person. I experience this type of boredom as a nagging feeling; it irritates and drains me.

There is another type of boredom that I experience as positive and healthy. This kind is felt on days when I have free time, such as when I can be at home and have no obligations. The day is open for possibilities and is waiting to be filled. I don't know what I will do even though so much can be done. Keeping hold of this feeling often leads to wonderful things. I suddenly get ideas, impulses, thoughts and inspiration. I feel intensely happy. I experience a rich, powerful source within myself. Work, cooking, baking, gardening, writing, doing sports or meeting up with someone – all of these things connect me with the world, and the world flows back to me in connection. This fulfils me in a wonderful way.

Children are also aware of these two types of boredom. A teacher who cannot keep children interested will have at least one child who is bored. The child yawns, disrupts, stares and daydreams. This child's mood can influence the entire class causing the connection between the subject and the teacher to disappear. At home, children who are bored and who do not receive the appropriate boundaries in which to handle this boredom alone, can influence the mood within the family. They whine and provoke other family members.

Children also know what healthy boredom is. This boredom helps them to arrive at their own rich, inner creative energy.

Children between six and nine months start to roll over. This gives them the ability to grasp a toy that is just slightly out of reach. We often see that children who are on the verge of taking the next step in their development whine and complain. There is something that they just can't do and it seems as if they know, somewhere deep inside, that this is the next step, that it is within reach. It is frustrating, but when the step is taken, there is a joyous moment of pride that they have been able to take this step all on their own.

Kindergartners experience moments when they just don't know what to do. There is no one to play with. Then, all of a sudden, they have found something and are lost in their own world. Older kindergartners experience this in the transition between kindergarten and school: the source of imagination is temporarily gone. Gardening, folding the washing, cooking and organising the shed can all help older kindergartners rediscover their imagination. Work that is enjoyed by adults stimulates the imagination of young children and leads them back to finding their own healthy play again.

Every time we as adults interfere in healthy boredom, we deprive children of the chance of taking the next developmental step independently. We deprive them of the experience that they can arrive at this moment on their own. We deprive them of being proud that they were able to endure their initial inability. By learning to endure, children develop resilience, tolerance for frustration and ingenuity. A strong inner world is developed into which they can always withdraw. They know that there is a wealth of possibilities hidden within themselves.

When parents respond to their child's boredom by offering to play with them, or telling them to watch television or play a game on their tablet, then the problem is solved from the outside. This is not a sustainable solution. Next time their child is bored, the child won't be able to look back to an earlier experience in which they endured the boredom and eventually found a solution to it themselves. This causes dependence on the outside world, instead of connecting them to their own rich inner world.

Parents who lovingly and respectfully give boundaries to boredom, allow their children to connect with their own healthy, inner source. In these moments we are effectively saying to our children: 'I trust your own inner resilience and power. I stand beside you and stay connected.' This asks us to be sensitive to our children, to have time and inner space to accept children who are bored, knowing that boredom has many sides. It also makes clear what our role as parent is. We are not someone who can be appealed to at all times. We are not the one who must save our children from boredom. We are an example of how people deal with boredom and how they process experiences in such a way that new ideas can be born. The only way to do this is if we give ourselves enough time, sleep, inner resolve and independence.

During his motoric development, a baby not only learns to roll onto his stomach, crawl, sit and walk, but he also learns to learn. He learns to keep himself busy independently, develop interest in something, try things, experiment. He learns to overcome difficulties. He gets to know the joy and satisfaction that arises when he succeeds, the result of his patience and perseverance. This is the foundation for the development of self-esteem and inner strength.

– Emmi Pikler

Let children solve their own problems

All healthy children develop strategies to deal with the problems they face in each phase of their lives. Parents who show their children that life challenges you to find creative solutions give their children a wonderful example. Children learn this best when in a protected environment. While lying in the playpen, a baby sees a block and wants to grab it. Thinking through the steps required to be able to grab this block is part of the child's development, just as learning to walk, ride a bike or clean their rooms by themselves are gifts for the development of a child's will. Every age presents new possibilities through which to learn how to solve problems and take risks.

Let children make mistakes

Children must be allowed to discover that making mistakes is part of life. Parents who show their children that it is OK to make mistakes and that it does not make sense to place the blame on someone else, teach them valuable qualities that they will draw on later in life. By experimenting, children experience what works and what doesn't and they learn that they are responsible for their mistakes. They discover new possibilities and what, perhaps, they will do differently next time.

Give children in-between time

Many children, and even adults, seem to live with the idea that everything they want they must have *NOW*. We live in a time in which 'in-between' time has all but disappeared. In-between time is the time between a desire and its fulfilment. It's wishing for something and waiting until your birthday or Christmas to receive it. It's learning to save up for something or waiting until you are older to be allowed to do something. Young children should learn that waiting is part of life and that they do not always get what they want. Learning to live with wishes that may or may not be granted gives them inner strength because it teaches them to deal with frustration and resistance. Learning to wait strengthens children's emotional power to resist, which can be a valuable quality to have in the challenges and temptations that lie ahead.

In-between time can be used in many different ways.

A nine-year-old child who announces that they've been invited to a friend's sleepover and they have to go because everyone else is going needs in-between time. A fair reaction by parents to such an announcement might be: 'Let me think about it. I'll let you know tomorrow.' The parent can then think it over, talk to their partner or someone else and ask other parents if their children are allowed to go. It's good to talk these things through with other parents, to share views and concerns and discuss the possibilities and impracticalities of letting a nine-year-old child go to a sleepover.

In-between time requires strength from parents and the ability to act with conscious presence of mind.

Give children undivided attention

Make way, make way, make way,
Make room, make room, make room,
We are in an incredible hurry
Make way, make way, make way,
Because we're almost too late
We only have a few minutes time.
We have to run, jump, fly, dive, fall, get up
    and keep going.
We can't stay now, we can't stay standing
    here any longer.

Another time perhaps
We will stay and sleep
And can then, if we really, really must,

Talk about this and that, football and lottery.
Well bye now, so long, be well.

– Herman van Veen

Undivided attention is when we give complete and utter attention to something with our whole being. This might be a telephone call, a walk on the beach or cooking a meal. Or it might be sitting quietly on your own with a cup of tea. Undivided attention is being fully present in the here and now. It requires inner peace, safety, trust and respect and in return it likewise gives trust, satisfaction, gratitude and connection.

Undivided attention is a precious thing when raising children, but it is something other than quality time. Quality time is usually defined as *doing* something with your child: going to a playpark or baking a cake. Undivided attention is about *being*: giving attention to what is here and now. Undivided attention does not mean that the parent should be on top of their child the whole day, as characterised by the helicopter parent we encountered earlier. Instead, it means that when we are with our children, we are with them fully in what we are doing together. Looking at a picture book with our smartphone in hand is not giving undivided attention. Our attention is then being shared with many other people who are not part of *this* moment, here and now. The child next to us holding the picture book *is* part of the moment. Undivided attention is being there fully for our children at least once a day, without looking at the time.

As a result of this, children feel loved and that they are

allowed to be there. Undivided attention is also letting children be when they are giving their undivided attention to a toy or a book, or whilst drawing or listening to music. Our interest in them and their activities is felt by children when we leave them be. Impinging on them disturbs the quality of their undivided attention.

Children who grow up in a home in which parents are conscious of undivided attention, feel that they are respected. They discover that undivided attention allows them to create an inner space in which peace, meaning and personal interpretation are experienced.

Undivided attention is also about teaching children to let their parents be when they say they are busy. The more parents teach this to their children, the clearer it is for them. However, children always want to feel that the invisible thread between them and their parents is still present. When parents do something for themselves, this does not mean that they are rejecting their children. Teaching children to respect undivided attention helps them to understand this.

EXAMPLE

A parent is working in the garden. The daughter wants to go to the pool but can't find her swimsuit. There are plenty of parents who catch themselves jumping up to help look for the missing suit. A child who can go to the pool independently can also look for a swimsuit independently.

EXAMPLE

A parent reads the newspaper and their young child, in imitation of the parent, wants to read with them. It is helpful, however, for the child to learn that there is a time for reading together and a time when the parent wants to read alone. The clearer these moments of undivided attention are the more they are respected by both parties.

Undivided attention creates. It opens a never-ending source. Through undivided attention we sharpen our awareness or find a deeper insight. We suddenly know what to do for our children, or we carry out some action and only realise later when looking back that it was the right thing to do.

By looking back at such golden moments, parents can start to understand what works in a certain situation for their children, something that may also work in another situation. By looking back at these moments at the end of the day, our thoughts accompany us into sleep, into worlds of imagination and inspiration. We can feel that raising children is not an uphill struggle that we face alone. We are given help. Everyone will give this help a different name. Some of us will associate it with our religion, some of us the world of ideas. Moments like this are a gift given to us thanks to undivided attention.

12. A SEVEN-STEP GUIDE TO SETTING APPROPRIATE BOUNDARIES

Whenever I give lectures on boundaries and speak to parents, they tell me how they wish there was a ready-made set of answers, or a simple recipe to follow that would tell them which boundaries to set, when to set them and how. This book is not a book of recipes, although like cooking the end product is the result of a step-by-step process: vegetables are sown and harvested, the consumer buys them, cleans and cooks them, they set the table and sit down to eat, and when they're finished they wash up. Raising children is a process made up of seven phases. Parents who want to establish loving boundaries as a foundation for their children's healthy development should consider the following seven life processes:

1. Observing
2. Connecting
3. Investigating
4. Deciding
5. Renewing
6. Applying
7. Creating

1. Observing

When we *observe*, we breathe in part of the world. We take something that is outside of us into us. Answers to our questions about raising children can often be found by watching children closely. In relation to this book this might mean that, as a parent, I observe that many babies are given pacifiers, or I observe that my thirteen-year-old boy has his mobile phone on and is on social media while doing his homework. I observe the feeling of irritation that I get from seeing my son use his mobile phone while doing his homework.

2. Connecting

What I observe is just *there*, but when I *connect* with what I observe then I take an interest in it. I approach it with an open mind. I connect with the observation and internalise it.

3. Investigating

The next step is to *investigate*. I process my observation. I break the observation down. As a parent, I do this by asking myself what a pacifier is and what it is used for. I also do this same exercise with my child's mobile phone. What is a mobile phone and what is its purpose? Who are you when you are thirteen years old and where are you in your development? What demands does homework make of a thirteen-year-old and should a mobile phone be part of that? As a parent, I analyse the observation completely.

4. Deciding

The above investigation helps parents to come to a *decision*. As a parent, ask yourself: what do I want and what don't I want? The answers to these questions will be determined by your view of humanity and your view on the development of your child.

In order to make a decision we must first go through the process of weighing up the pros and cons. Only then can we find the middle way, much like finding the right balance on a scale. If my child's classmates all have mobile phones, I might not want my child to feel left out. But I might also see a mobile phone as an expensive investment. Who will pay for the pre-paid card or monthly bill? As a parent, I know that a thirteen-year-old has difficulty planning and focusing on homework. Is a mobile phone conducive to doing homework? By taking the time to ask these questions you can arrive at properly considered answers.

5. Renewing

As a parent, I want to make decisions that contribute to a sustainable relationship with my children and invest in a lasting, loving upbringing. After all, raising children is a long-term investment. Parents are challenged to grow with the development of their children, thereby assessing new questions that arise. Parenting should not become fixed or static; it is a process which is continually *renewed* through practice.

6. Applying

By internalising a question, it becomes possible for a parent to come to a well-thought-out decision or answer. The parent can then *apply* a boundary with inner strength because the heart, in which love abides, has weighed the possibilities.

7. Creating

Creating is the crown that sits on top of this process. As a parent I have made a decision: I decide not to give my child a pacifier, but sucking a thumb is fine. Or I tell my thirteen-year-old that they can have a mobile phone but they will have to pay for the pre-paid card out of their pocket money. The child may not be happy with the decision, but the decision shows I-power. I-power that children want to lovingly imitate, each according to their own stage of development.

Boundaries that are given time to be considered and put into place according to the process outlined above – a process that does not drain but nourishes us and allows us to grow – will help parents create loving spaces in which to raise children. Thankfully, not all questions need to go through this process. With experience, an inner trust grows in parents that allows us to apply our thoughts and decisions more and more consciously.

13. TWELVE GOLDEN WORDS

Give your child love, without accepting everything. And be convinced that boundaries are not restrictions.

– Steven Pont

Parents who always value these twelve key aspects of life will raise children who stand tall in later life: independent, authentic, protected and protecting, bound in solidarity with themselves and the world around them.

Rest

To be at rest, or at peace, means to be still. It means being attentive to what is – in other words, being present. Rest is not boring, in fact, it can be dynamic.

Rest plays an essential part in bringing up children, or during self-education. 'The grass does not grow faster if you pull on it' is an apt phrase translated from Dutch. Everything that is organic needs time to develop. The opposite of this is haste. Haste is not effective when raising children. As parents, we only make things difficult for ourselves if we raise children in haste. Rest gives presence of mind; we are there with our children with complete attention. People around us also notice and appreciate it. Life blossoms when there is rest and peace.

Regularity

Regularity and rhythm are closely connected. A family that has a rhythm, a regular routine, creates a strong foundation and supporting structure for their children. There may be times when life overflows, but there is always a regular pattern of life to return to.

EXAMPLE

A family is on holiday at a farm, which bustles with activity until late in the evening: the goats need to be brought to a different field, the cats need to be fed, and the children are allowed to help, alongside new friends they have made. Dinner is not always eaten at the table and everyone goes to bed past their usual bedtime. At the end of the holiday, the children are easily irritated. The parents know that this is because the rhythm of the daily life that the children are used to has been temporarily lost. Through this understanding, the parents can accept the irritations and change them into something positive, saying to their children, 'We've had a wonderful holiday on the farm! You all worked so hard, played so well and went to bed late. When we are home, we'll all go to bed on time again. Then we won't get angry with each other so easily any more.'

Cleanliness

Cleanliness in a literal sense is not just about how much time parents spend cleaning their house. A clean house has to do with attention to maintenance and hygiene, so that rooms such as the bathroom and the kitchen are pleasant spaces.

Cleanliness in a figurative sense means 'clean on the inside': how you see yourself, your children and everyone who has a part in your children's life. It has to do with cleaning up difficult aspects from your own childhood.

Cleanliness also has to do with how parents interact. Every relationship has its problems. In every family, there are moments when parents have different ideas about raising their children. This relationship remains 'clean' if the parents do not ignore each other but discuss the problems at a suitable moment when there is time, attention and rest. It can be instructive for children to see their parents argue and make up if the arguments show how their parents stay connected even when they disagree. Good communication is the key to this.

Enough

Children are continually growing, not just physically but mentally and emotionally as well. At around two-and-a-half years of age, their imaginative powers start to develop. At around seven years of age many of these powers change into faculties for academic learning. Their emotional life also starts to develop and it is the parent's task to guide this emotional development, to feed it where needed but also to curb it where necessary. They must slow things down and apply the brake. For example, children of this age still need to be told when bedtime is because they haven't developed to the point where they can decide it independently. They need to learn how many ice creams are enough on a summer's day. Parents apply the brake to allow their children to continue safely on a healthy path.

Direction

Children need parents who can guide them through the storms of life, who can show them how things are done in the culture into which they have been born, and who know that children want to follow and imitate an authoritative figure. They need parents who are not afraid to take a stance and decide which path to take. Children need their parents to make decisions that fit them and the family, even if these decisions are not the popular choice.

Respect

Respect is the purest form of love.

— Emmi Pikler

Respect in the context of parenting means that parents recognise and appreciate the authenticity of their children. They must accept that their children are not clones of themselves but independent beings. Respect also has to do with integrity, with the parents living according to the values of society so that, through imitation, children can begin to learn about them.

Roles

All people are equal, no life is more important than any other. But whilst parents and children are equal as human beings, they are not equal in other ways. Parents are older and have more life experience: they can relate cause and effect; they know that eating three ice creams will make them feel sick, and they have a more strongly developed sense of self, or I-power. Both qualities allow them to navigate life and accept responsibility for their choices; their experiences have allowed them to build up inner foundations.

Parents know that life goes through developmental phases and that children must develop unique qualities during each phase, such as learning to wait, holding back, developing resilience, or learning to stand up for themselves. Three year olds cannot decide what they want on their sandwich yet, whether cheese, ham or peanut butter; fifteen year olds should not have to decide if their curfew is at midnight or 10 pm. Parents narrow the choices down for a three-year-old to two possibilities, either cheese or peanut butter; curfew between 10 pm and 10.15 pm for a fifteen-year-old.

It is the role of parents to guide while always keeping the whole child in mind. Parents lead, guide, adjust, watch, wait, trust. Children meanwhile trust that the direction taken has been thought out lovingly. Parents give the children enough room to make choices for which they are ready at the right time.

Healthy, loving boundaries have everything to do with knowing who has which role. Conflicts usually arise between parents and children if these roles are not clear. Parents are not playmates, entertainers or clowns, nor are they the children's slaves.

Response

> If listening to react
> Changes into listening to understand
> Then real contact is made.
>
> – Dalai Lama

As parents we wait with baited breath until our newborn responds to us, and the first smile makes all those sleepless nights worthwhile.

Response grows together with the relationship between parent and child: children give off signals, parents respond and so on. Response also has to do with how parents and children react to each other. How do the parents expect their children to react? What kind of behaviour do parents demonstrate to their children when it comes to response and reciprocity? Parents who do not want their children to swear but who swear all the time themselves should not be surprised if their children imitate them. This is also a form of response.

Space

Space, in the context of healthy, loving boundaries, refers to space within which children feel safe to move around and develop freely. Parents should search for the right amount of space for each developmental phase. What fits now, at this time, at this age, for this child?

Space also refers to the space parents need as individuals and as a couple in order to develop and maintain their relationship.

Elasticity

Elastic stretches, but elastic that is kept taut for too long loses its strength. For parents to remain full of energy, the connection with their children must remain intact, but at the same time they must ensure that the bond is not too taut or too loose. A symbiotic relationship between mother and child during pregnancy and the first year is healthy but it slowly decreases as the child grows so that they can become independent beings.

Loving, healthy boundaries are elastic when needed, befitting the situation or developmental phase of the child. They are not rigid.

Relationships

Raising children means having relationships on many different levels. First of all, it means having a healthy relationship with yourself as a human being, as a partner in a relationship and as a parent for your children. It also means having a relationship with the teachers at your children's school or other adults who are associated with your children. If parents are separated it is important that they maintain an amicable relationship if this is at all possible.

But is also means caring for relationships with the invisible world, which children experience in a very real way. Toddlers and kindergartners can easily talk to invisible friends, their dolls or stuffed animals. Young children are sometimes afraid to say something to adults but will confide in a puppet held by an adult. I call all these examples of 'the other world that participates'. This is the magical world, the world of imagination and inspiration, the world of elemental beings and angels and everything else we cannot see with our eyes but can experience with our hearts.

Backbone

The last word that should accompany you on your journey is backbone. Our backbone is made up of many different vertebrae that work together and thus allow a human being to stand tall and straight with two feet on the ground, strong between heaven and earth. Parents who show their children loving boundaries, but do not neglect their own self-development, build a strong inner backbone. This book has discussed various subjects that will help parents guide their children towards growing into healthy human beings with strong, flexible backbones: able to both take a stance on something and bend when asked.

We can think of this backbone like the mast of a boat. The mast is rigged with sails that fill with wind and carry the boat over the seas of life towards its goal. The mast should be just the right size for the boat and the sails, and the boat should be able to carry the mast and sails. While sailing, the parents adjust the size of the mast and sails. When circumstances change – say the weather turns out worse than expected – then the sails must be adjusgted again. Boundaries, like the sails, should not be set too tight nor too loose, but just right.

ACKNOWLEDGEMENTS

This book has come about as a result of the many conversations I've had with parents and with those who have asked me to write down what I talk about in my lectures.

I would like to thank all the children, parents, teachers and other educators whom I have met during my research on the subject of boundaries, and everyone from whom I've learned through conversations, opinions, confrontations and encounters. I would like to thank my family for their love and support.

In particular I would like to thank Willem de Jong for permission to cite from his work on boundaries.

BIBLIOGRAPHY

Bom, P and Huber, M. (2008) *Baby's First Year: Growth and Development from 0 to 12 Months*, Floris Books, Edinburgh.

Bom, P and Huber, M. (2009) *Toddler Years: Growth and Development from 1 to 4 Years*, Floris Books, Edinburgh.

Köhler, H. (2013) *Difficult Children: There Is No Such Thing: An Appeal for the Transformation of Educational Thinking*, Awsna Publications, US

Jong, W. de (2013) 'Allers voor je kind: Problematische verwenning maakt meer stuk dan je life is.' *Orthopedagogiek: Onderzoek en Praktick*. 52 (10, 447-456). Garant.

Lievegoed, B. (2005) *Phases of Childhood: Growing in Body, Soul and Spirit*, Floris Books, Edinburgh.

Marano, H. E. (2008) *A Nation of Wimps: The High Cost of Invasive* Schoorel, E. (2014) *First Seven Years: Physiology of Childhood*, Rudolf Steiner College Press, USA.

Soesman, A. (2006) *Our Twelve Senses: How Healthy Senses Refresh the Soul*, Hawthorn Press, UK.

Steiner, R. (2007) *Balance in Teaching*, SteinerBooks, US.

—, (1996) *The Education of the Child and Early Lectures on Education*, Anthroposophic Press, New York.

—, (1996) *The Foundations of Human Experience*, Anthroposophic Press, New York.

—, (2003) *Soul Economy, Body, Soul and Spirit in Waldorf Education*, SteinerBooks, US.

—, (2004) *The Spiritual Ground of Education*, SteinerBooks, US.